GIRL WORLD

A Real Girl's Guide to Surviving Girl Wars, Gossip, Cliques and Boys.

Theresa Cheung

a division of Hodder Headline Limited

© Hodder Children's Books 2005
Illustration copyright © Pesky Kids 2005

Published in Great Britain in 2005
by Hodder Children's Books

Editor: Hayley Leach
Design by Don Martin
Cover design: Hodder Children's Books

10 9 8 7 6 5 4 3 2 1

ISBN: 0340884479

Printed by Bookmarque Ltd, Croydon, Surrey

The paper and board used in this paperback by Hodder Children's Books
are natural recyclable products made from wood grown in sustainable
forests. The manufacturing processes conform to the environmental
regulations of the country of origin.

Hodder Children's Books
a division of Hodder Headline Limited
338 Euston Road
London NW1 3BH

Contents

Introduction

The
lunch tray
moment

You have a close group of girlfriends, but one day in the queue for lunch one of them tells you that another friend is saying mean things about you. Your face feels hot; you can feel everyone looking at you. Thoughts race through your head. What did you do? Why is she mad at you? Are your friends going to back you up or side with her? All of a sudden, you feel an icy stab of fear as you stand there clutching your blue plastic tray and you wonder: *Where am I going to sit for lunch?*

It's wonderful when you fit in with Girl World, but it's terrifying when you don't. That's where this book can help. It takes you inside the secret world of girls' friendships and gives you the low-down on what's happening in today's tough Girl World, from gossip and cliques to boys and body image.

Fitting in with your girlfriends is a big deal. There are standards, after all: things you need to do to look right and to fit in. But who enforces these standards? Films? Teen magazines? No, it's your girlfriends themselves. Like big sisters, they watch your every move – what you wear, how you look, which boys you're interested in and how you act. You're getting daily lessons about what's in and what's out, what's hot and what's not from your friends. You don't watch MTV or read teen magazines by yourself. You watch and read them with your girlfriends.

I used to be a schoolteacher and counsellor (and survivor from an all girls' school), and I've listened to hundreds of girls talk about their friends. Girlfriends and cliques have a lot of power to shape what you wear and say, how you feel about school, how you respond to boys, and how you feel about yourself. Forget sugar and spice, I've seen how mean girls can be to each other and how girls can bully other girls. In this book I'll show you how to gather the girl power you need to survive and thrive, so that when those lunch tray moments happen – and believe me, they happen to us all – you'll be able to get through the day with style.

Chapter one

Girl world

Ms Brown, an enthusiastic trainee drama teacher, tells the girls in year 9 to form a circle. She wonders why this takes so much time, and she just doesn't realise that it's a big thing for the girls: who will stand next to who? As the girls dither, Ms Brown gets angry and shouts at them: 'Get your act together now!' Then something unimaginable happens. Chloe, the coolest girl in the class, just happens to be standing next to Sally, the class loser. What will happen? Will Chloe let Sally hold her hand? As they edge closer Chloe accidentally brushes against Sally. Chloe jumps away as if she's just been stung by a bee. All the girls giggle, and Sally pretends to giggle too.

Welcome to Girl World. Why is Chloe being so mean? Why does Sally think she has to pretend it's funny too? Why is everyone siding with Chloe? Why doesn't the teacher get it? Read on for the answers.

No matter how many friends you have, the chances are you'll run into problems with popularity at some point. Perhaps your friends decide that you no longer fit in, or you're teased for wearing the wrong outfit or having the wrong friend. Or maybe you've got stuck with a reputation you can't shake, or you feel you have to be like your friends in order to be liked. Whatever the reason, sooner or later you'll be hurt in some way by your girlfriends.

For better or for worse, it's your close girlfriends who teach you volumes about friendship, support, understanding and power. On a daily basis you learn what kind of girl you have to be, to be accepted by your friends. And even though you may not realise it, what you learn will influence everything from your choice of boyfriend to the quality of your schoolwork, the clothes you wear, the people you mix with, the things you say and do, and the woman you will one day become.

Nothing's better than your close group of friends, right? You hang around with them, share secrets with them, have fun with them and feel supported by them. But what about the other side of things? You've probably also seen the backbiting,

gossip and meanness in your group of friends. Maybe some of it was directed at you. Let's face it, even if you haven't met any mean girls in person, they exist in every school. And sadly they often tend to be the so-called 'popular' girls or 'cool' girls with the most influence.

Here's what some girls said about the 'cool' girls in their school. Do any of these comments sound familiar?

◇◇◇ 'I'm scared of them.'

◇◇◇ 'They're mean and make me feel like I'm nothing.'

◇◇◇ 'They've got all the power and always get their way.'

◇◇◇ 'I'd like to stand up to them but know they'll make fun of me.'

It may seem like you are powerless and there is nothing you can do when mean girls target or exclude you, but this isn't the case. There's a whole lot you can do!

◇ Fighting talk

Don't panic. When girls ignore or pick on other girls, you have the power to learn from it and turn it to your advantage. Don't think you can't do it. Of course you can. The chapters that follow will guide and support you.

You are special. There is no one quite like you with your heart, your brains and your style. You have loads of potential and a terrific future ahead of you. Don't let anyone stop you in your quest to be the best that you can be.

◇ Understanding mean girl behaviour

In the next few chapters we'll take a look at the various types of mean girl behaviour. You'll learn what makes mean girls tick and why they do what they do. Then you'll use what you've learned so that next time you won't get pushed around or intimidated.

As you read, bear in mind that some mean girl behaviour isn't immediately obvious. It can be hidden with a smile. It can even look attractive. But if you want to get on top of the situation, it's important to be able to spot the not-so-nice ways of treating other girls – whether it's sneaky, hidden, or out in the open.

A word of caution: When we discuss mean girl behaviour, we're talking about how a girl *acts,* not what she *is.* Everyone has a good side, even the school bully, and everyone has many sides to their personality. A girl can switch roles from one year – or one month – to the next. She might act differently

when a new student arrives or when her body
changes and she looks different from other girls.

Don't forget to turn the spotlight on yourself. No girl
is perfect, including you. You may have said or done
things that are wrong and hurtful. In your desire to fit
in and be 'cool', are you sometimes guilty of mean
girl behaviour too?

Chapter two

The
scary chick

We'll plunge right in with the scariest chick of them all: the bully. This girl is tough and mean. She's usually part of a group but is just as mean when she's alone. She makes fun of people who are weaker, smaller or cleverer than she is. Perhaps you've seen her – giving hateful looks to other girls, trashing other people's bags or books, whispering threats as you walk past her or even pushing you over when she thinks no one else is looking.

 'I don't even know this girl, but she is so mean to me. Whenever we pass on the stairs she scratches me with her fingernails. It's got so bad that I hide and wait until she has gone to her next class, and then I go and get into trouble with my teacher for

being late. I've tried to tell my mum, but she says I need to toughen up.'
Monica, 14

'For no reason at all, I get picked on. It's making my life hell. It seems just the fact that I'm breathing is enough for her to push and elbow me around every chance she gets. Why does she hate me so much?'
Nina, 13

The scary chick – the bully – has it in for girls like you. She wants to hurt you. It may get so bad that you don't want to go to school anymore because you are so scared of her. She can pop up anytime and turn your day into a nightmare. Maybe it's small, like calling you names as you walk down the corridor, or large, like pushing you over so you fall and get hurt. Or maybe she just threatens to do something, and you feel sick to your stomach just thinking about it. When the scary chick is around, you can't enjoy life. Nowhere seems safe.

The scary chick is one of the hardest mean girls to handle because of her aggressive behaviour. Bullying is wrong – it's as simple as that – and if it's allowed to continue it gets worse. Bullying has to stop, and maybe you are the person who can help to stop it.

There is no magic formula to make the scary chick go away, but there are things you can do to stop her from ruining your life. These things aren't complicated, but you will have to do one thing: find your courage and stop being a victim.

When you bump into the bully and she blocks your way, what do you do?

1. Run away in tears.

2. Try to get on her good side with flattery.

3. Push her aside and start a fight.

4. Stand your ground and confront her calmly. If she doesn't budge, take a different route.

If you chose the first answer, you are letting the bully walk all over you. If you chose the second, you are making things worse for you and for other girls. If you chose the third, you are in danger of becoming more and more like the bully, and that's no way to solve the problem. If you chose the final answer, you are in control of the situation and not allowing things to get on top of you. Option four is definitely the best choice to make but possibly the most difficult. Read on to find out how to deal with the bully.

The bullying problem is spreading, and it won't go away overnight. Your school may be more used to dealing with boys who are violent troublemakers than with girls, but increasingly schools are becoming aware that striking out with words can be just as damaging as a punch in the stomach. They are waking up to the fact that girls can be bullies too, so don't feel that you are alone if a scary chick has made you her target.

Bullying can turn nice girls into bullies themselves. It's a vicious circle, so what can you do to stop the scary chicks taking over?

◇ Coping with the scary chick

First of all, remind yourself that you are not the cause of the bully's problems, even if she makes you think you are. A lot of bullies have been abused or neglected, and they are taking their hurt out on you.

 This doesn't excuse what they do, but it might help you to understand them better. Bullies often feel insecure and think no one loves them. They're trying to make others feel as bad as they do.

What can you do to cope with the bully? Avoiding her is one option until you figure out how to deal with the situation. Stay away from the places where you know she hangs around until you feel ready to cope with her. Try to change your attitude. Come to school feeling strong instead of scared. Have a few comments ready when she confronts you, such as: 'Sorry if you're having a bad day today but there's no reason to take it out on me.' Then step around her and carry on.

Every time a girl is mean to you it's okay to feel hurt, angry, scared or all three. But the next time it happens, think about how you handled it. Did you

walk away? Did you talk back? How did it make you
feel? Then, when you get a chance to be alone, replay
the event in your mind and think about
ways you could have handled it
differently or better. Keep these
things in mind if it happens again.

Stand up for yourself. Stay strong. Most
bullies are cowards. Once she sees that you are
prepared to take a stand, the chances are she'll back
off. If she doesn't, then it's *absolutely
crucial* that you ask for help from your
parents and from your teachers. If you feel
you can't do that, you owe it to yourself to phone one
of the free and confidential helplines listed in the
Useful Contacts section on page 123 for
advice. You'll also find lots more tips on
how to stand up for yourself in the rest of
this book, so keep reading!

◇ **Bad-attitude days**

We all have them – days when we get up on the
wrong side of the bed or when we feel like slamming
doors or lashing out at others. The trouble is, having a
bad day and taking it out on someone else is just like

being a bully yourself. So how can you handle those mad feelings?

Well, you don't take it out on other people, like a bully does. Warn other people that you are having a bad day and you'll chat tomorrow. Say as little as you can until you get home, then have a long warm bath, put on your favourite music and hug your pillow. As the bad  feelings fade, plan something you like – like a shopping trip or a swim at the local pool.

And remember, just because you feel angry doesn't mean you have to act angry. Don't ruin your own day! Nobody but you is in charge of the way you feel. Sometimes we all feel rough – but you don't have to make those bad feelings last for long. You're the one in control.

Chapter three

The
It girl

This girl seems to have everything. She has the best parties, the coolest friends, the cutest boyfriends, the perfect look – and the teachers adore her. She can get away with anything. With a word or a glance, she can make or break your day, depending on her mood.

◇◇◇ 'There's a girl in my class who makes me feel like I'm dirt. She thinks she's so cool because her parents are rich and live abroad. She's always bragging about the holidays she has, the boys she dates, the grown-up things she does and the hundreds of parties she's invited to. I hate her. She's such a spoiled brat.'
Zoe, 12

◇◇◇ 'She bosses me around. Nothing I do, or wear, or say is right. She has to get her way in everything. She tells me the things she does with boys – things that I don't want to hear. I put up with it because when she ignores me it's horrible, horrible. I feel so left out and alone.' *Laura, 13*

The It girl is popular because she looks like she's in control. She seems very grown-up. Think of a cross between the vain, cruel stepmother in Snow White and the beautiful but shallow Barbie. With her confidence, money and ability to manipulate, this girl reigns supreme over other girls. She weakens their friendships with others so that she can strengthen her own power. She's the top cat with an answer for everything, and she can silence other girls (and boys) with a look. Her friends always do what she wants, she likes to be the centre of attention, she can argue anyone down, even teachers, and she's charming to adults. You feel edgy around her, but she can make you feel like the chosen one if she decides to spend time with you.

There is always at least one It girl in a group of girlfriends. When she's around, do you turn into a meek lamb, or do you tell her what the score is? Let's find out. Do you:

1. Keep out of her way?

2. Go along with her and do everything she says?

3. Stand up to her?

4. Treat her the same way as everyone else?

If you chose number one, the It girl is intimidating you and stopping you being the person you want to be. If you chose number two, you are acting like the It girl's slave. You are living your life to please her. If you chose number three, you have a strong attitude, but you'll also have to face the not-so-pleasant consequences of a war with the It girl. If you chose number four, you are an independent-minded girl who is cool, calm and collected. Option four is definitely the best choice!

◇ How to keep your cool

To keep your cool, first of all remind yourself that, like the bully, the It girl has problems that have nothing to do with you. There's a big emptiness inside her and she's trying to fill it with material things like clothes or by controlling the lives of her friends. She feels insecure and afraid and tries to make herself feel better at your expense.

Take her clothes for example. In Girl World, clothes and the way you look are major status symbols. Wearing the most fashionable clothes makes the It girl feel and act superior to other girls who don't dress in the best gear. But next time she makes you feel you aren't good enough or don't look right, just think that maybe it's her, not you, who is hurting on the inside.

You could try being a friend to her – not a doormat but a real friend. She might need one. Deep down there may be a nice girl waiting to get out.

Another way to keep her from getting the upper hand is to know, deep down, that you are just as good as she, or anybody else, is. Stop making yourself invisible around her. Let your own light shine! We all feel bad about ourselves from time to time, but you don't have to let those feelings continue. Try turning them around. Focus instead on something good about yourself – and then see how little you care about what she thinks of you.

Try being prepared. Have a few responses ready. If she puts you down, say 'You must be having a really tough day.' When she brags about something to you, say 'I'm glad you did so well.' Always be friendly and genuine with everyone. Teach her to respect you by the example you set.

◇ If you're the It girl...

Finally, should you ever find any snobby feelings within yourself, stop them dead in their tracks. Feeling superior to other people for whatever reason won't help anyone – and it's one of the fastest ways to lose friends.

Chapter four

The
sidekick

The sidekick is the second-in-command, the girl who's closest to either the It girl or the scary chick. She'll back her 'best friend' no matter what because she gets all her confidence from hanging around with the 'cool' girls. She dresses the same as them, acts the same and talks the same. You must have seen her. Where the top cat is, she isn't far behind. Together they seem unbeatable. They usually silence (or bully) other girls to get what they what. But remember this: the It girl or bully can pick up any old sidekick they want, but the sidekick just doesn't have the same ability to make you feel small without the bully by her side.

When she's with the It girl or scary chick, the sidekick can be just as cruel. It's bad enough when one girl goes out of her way to make your life a misery, but when two girls do, you feel like a walking target.

'At first it was just Jenny who was making fun of me, but now it's Alice too. When it was just one person it wasn't too bad, I could deal with it, but now I feel completely alone. How can I be sure that the other girls in the class won't join them?

They've got the coolest clothes, the cutest
boyfriends, and the teachers on their side.
What have I got to offer? A secondhand uniform,
no boyfriend and a great big zit on my nose.'
Victoria, 12

It's horrible when two girls unite in hatred against
you, ignore you, call you names or even worse,
threaten you with violence. Suddenly you're afraid
and you think no one is ever going to really like you.
You feel vulnerable and very alone.

**Picture the scene: you are
walking home from school, and
the bully and her sidekick are
walking behind you. You can hear
them making rude comments
about you behind your back.
Do you:**

1. Run away as fast as you can?

2. Feel flattered that they are walking
with you and beg to join them?

3. Shout rude comments back?

4. Ignore them, hold your head high and
walk home at your normal pace?

The first three responses won't help anyone, least of all you, but number four will. If you refuse to let these two get to you, you can show them that you are a strong person who won't be intimidated. This approach is by far the best, because the mean chicks won't be getting what they're looking for. They're trying to show off their power, and if they don't get the reaction they want, they're not going to bother next time.

◇ Coping with the sidekick

When two girls gang up against you once it's bad enough, but what if it goes on for months? Here's what you need to know.

The sidekick does what she does because she's lonely. She will do anything to have a friend – even hurt other girls. By herself she has no power. She is nowhere near as mean without the It girl or the bully

to back her up. She thinks she's getting a lot from being friends with her, but you can bet she's losing a lot – like her personality. If she sticks around the bully or the It girl for too long, she may forget she even has her own opinion. When you see her with her so-called friend, act in the same way as you would act towards the bully or It girl alone.

But what if you catch her alone? The chances are that the sidekick is being pushed around by her first-in-command and she is not as happy as she looks. Try to find ways to get to know her and perhaps even become her friend. You may be surprised to find that there is a nice person hiding behind the show.

◇ A herd of sheep

Sometimes there's just one sidekick in your class, but often there are three or four, or maybe a whole group hanging around with the It girl or the bully. When they are alone they aren't too bad, but put them with their clique and they can be terrifying.

If you're scared of a group of girls who all act the same, think of them another way – as girls who are very scared on the inside. They're looking for safety in numbers. They aren't brave enough to develop their own style. Why should you be intimidated by people who can't stand on their own two feet?

◇ If you're the sidekick ...

Yes, every friendship group involves a certain amount of going along with the pack. You've probably been pressured by your friends at some point to fit in, but always be careful with this kind of pressure. At first it may only be about what you can and cannot wear, but then it might be about who you can and cannot date, or you might even have to be cruel to other girls to fit in. That's not okay.

There's one problem, you see, with following the herd – it usually leads downhill. Don't get caught up in this kind of game. Focus on yourself – on your talents and your future. Rather than spending your energy on trying to please or conform, be the strong girl and say no to what doesn't work for you.

Chapter five

The
gossip

The gossip seems to be everywhere. She has all the latest news about everyone and everything. She's cute and loves to talk when she wants to find something out from you, but once she gets what she wants – oh, dear. This girl can be trouble. You told her, in confidence, that you fancy the new maths teacher, and now it's all over the school and everyone is smirking at you as you head to your lesson.

'I have this friend who is so nice to my face and says such good things. Then I hear from my sister that she says really disgusting things about me behind my back. Everything I say or do is exaggerated. But whenever I confront her she just smiles sweetly and acts so innocent.'
Lara, 14

The gossip always has lots to talk about, but 99 per cent of the time what she says is nasty. Plus, it's never about her – it's always about someone else. The big shame is that there is a lot to like about her – she's chatty, she's fun, she makes you feel special and best of all she loves to listen. But BEWARE. Though it may seem like she is interested in you and willing to offer advice about your boyfriend troubles or your weight worries, you may find that by lunchtime the whole school knows about your problems.

Gossip isn't all bad – sharing news is
what makes the world go round –
but it turns bad when the gossip is
untrue or vicious or when it's told
to make someone else look bad.

Have you ever had a friend who acts nice until she
hears what she wants and then behind your back tells
others what you told her in secret? When someone
gossips about things that you really want to keep
private, it's one of the worst things that can happen
to you. It can make you feel like you can't trust
anyone ever again.

◇◇◇ 'I trusted Elizabeth and had no idea what she was
really like. I told her everything – how worried I
was about starting my periods late, the arguments
I have with mum, what I think of the other girls
in my class. When I found out that she had gone
behind my back and told all the girls exactly what
I thought of them, I was gutted. I don't think
I can ever have a really close friend again. It's
too risky.'
Lily, 16

Every girl gets gossiped about at some time in her life, and let's face it, every girl gossips. No one is innocent here. Just bear in mind that spreading news that you know should be private is cowardly. You're trying to make yourself look better than someone else. With this kind of gossip, you can do serious damage.

How gossip-proof are you?
Picture the scene: the gossip sits down with you at lesson break and tells you she's just heard the latest dirt on Claire, a quiet girl you sometimes talk to. Do you:

1. Listen and giggle to make sure you aren't the gossip's next target?

2. Join in anxiously with the conversation?

3. Join in the gossip and share some of your own?

4. Say no thank you. Claire will tell you if there is something you need to know?

If you chose number one, you are letting the gossip walk all over you. If you chose number two, you will do anything to win other people's approval, even at the expense of your friends. If you chose number three, you are as bad as the gossip herself. But if you chose number four, people know where they stand with you. You are an honest, decent girl and incredibly strong. There is nothing more powerful than saying no to nasty gossip.

◇ Coping with the gossip

The gossip craves attention, and maybe there is nobody to listen to her at home. Understand where she's coming from. She is desperate to feel important, and so she is grabbing at anything. Try to see the good in her. She probably is a nice person who just needs to find an outlet for her skills. She loves to pick up news, so maybe you could suggest that she go into journalism!

If you find out you've been gossiped about, don't let it get to you. Laugh it off. Keep your cool. Let the gossip know that you heard what she's been saying about you, and tell her that if you needed a publicity manager you'd get one for yourself. Above all, stop giving her personal details. If she shared intimate personal details that you asked to be kept secret, put an end to the friendship. It's better not to have any friends than ones you can't trust. And remember the rumour mill at school goes faster than the speed of light. People will soon forget about you and move on to the next juicy bit of news.

◇ Are you guilty of gossiping?

We all pass on rumours, exaggerate from time to time. It gives us a thrill. But think about your actions. How do you really feel when you gossip – powerful or petty? We gossip to feel powerful, but most likely we end up feeling petty instead. If you catch yourself gossiping, stop and think about the time you were hurt when people talked about you. Why would you want someone else to feel that way?

If gossip becomes an everyday ritual, you'd better watch out; you are in danger of becoming petty, spiteful, cruel, and sneaky, and none of these words are good ones, are they? So the next time you are tempted to spill the beans or listen to juicy gossip, don't give in. Do something more constructive with your time. If you want to spread rumours make sure they aren't hurtful ones, and if you hear rumours being spread about someone else, don't join in. Offer your support to the person being affected by it instead.

Chapter six

The
back-stabber

Being let down by your girlfriend can be horrible. One minute she's your best mate, and the next she's gone off with a new friend and dumped you. Or maybe she flirts with a boy she knows you fancy or she talks about you behind your back. You thought you could trust her but you are beginning to realise that you've been stabbed in the back.

◇◇◇ 'The last person I expected to go behind my back – I loved that girl. She was my best friend, and she knew everything about me. Every time I think about her I feel sick.'
Mandy, 13

The back-stabber is sneaky, and she plays her part so well you never suspect her. She's your best friend, like a sister. She's someone you feel you can share

everything with. She's the friend you rely on the most and the one you turn to when things go wrong. The bond of your friendship is sacred. Then one day out of the blue you are shocked to discover that she has broken that trust. She talked about you behind your back or she simply lost interest in you. The pain and agony cannot be put into words.

Picture the scene: you find out that your best friend is chasing your boyfriend. Do you:

1. Lie low until the whole thing blows over, because you are too hurt to face your friend?

2. Blame your boyfriend?

3. Dump your boyfriend and dump your friend and let everyone know how devious they have been?

4. Get the facts right. Find out exactly what went on and then make your decision. If your friend did go behind your back, tell her she has hurt you and broken your trust and things may never be the same between you?

If you chose answer number one, sooner or later you are going to have to learn that hiding from problems never solves anything. If you chose number two, ask yourself why you are clinging to a friend you can't trust. Don't you deserve better? If you chose number three, it will feel good to give as good as you got, but this isn't the way to win. If you chose number four, you're on the right track. You are facing up to the traitor and giving her an ultimatum – be a better friend or she may lose you forever.

◇ Coping with the back-stabber

Keep this in mind: the back-stabber has often been let down herself by people she cares about, but she hasn't learned from the experience. She's repeating it instead. She doesn't know what real friendship is, so for the time being stay away from her. Perhaps in time you will be able to be friends again, but think long and hard before you leap. To find out if your friendship is worth saving, have a serious talk with your 'friend'. If she apologises and seems genuinely sorry, this is a good sign. After more talking and some time apart, you might be able to trust her again. Make sure you learn from the experience. If you've been stabbed in the back this shouldn't mean that you can take it out on other people and be a back-stabber yourself.

Be resilient when bad things happen to you. Don't let being disappointed by someone stop you or make you believe bad things about yourself. Whatever you do, don't become cynical or turn your back on other girls. Try to think of betrayal as an important lesson to learn about friendship.

Understand that no matter how hurt you feel by the back-stabber, you will get over it. It won't be easy to trust anyone after such a letdown, but every time you bounce back from a fall, you are growing in strength and power. There are real friends out there – it's just a matter of finding them, chapter twelve will show you how. Remember that real friendship takes time and good judgement. Beware of confiding in friends too early. Take your time. Trust your instincts; they are usually your best guide.

◇ If you're the back-stabber ...

Don't let what the back-stabber did turn you into someone your friends can't trust. Try to remember that feeling conflicting emotions about yourself and your friends is normal and very human. Even the fact that you often

feel jealous of your friends or sometimes wish bad things on them is normal. You are growing up, and your emotions are too, so you can expect a bumpy ride along the way. If you find that unfriendly thoughts come into your mind, don't give in to them. Do your best to replace them with peaceful, friendly ones. Find an outlet for your mean thoughts – take a walk, write in a diary – and then forget about them.

Chapter seven

The joker

In many ways the joker is worse than all the other mean girls we've mentioned so far. Like the back-stabber, she is sneaky so you may have no idea who she is. She could be your best friend or just someone you are used to seeing around.

❖❖❖ 'I had a problem with eating last year. I was overweight but then decided to start eating more healthily. I'm a better weight now. Some time ago we did a lesson on nutrition, and I got top marks when I wrote an essay on it. Ever since, the girls in my class have called me Ms Nutrition, but my best friend changed that into Ms Malnutrition. Now that's what I'm known as wherever I go. I try to laugh it off, but it really hurts me.'
Sally, 15

The joker is a girlfriend who likes to have fun at your expense. More often than not, her joking can turn into teasing or taunting. Often you have no idea if she is just having a laugh or being really cruel. It may start off harmlessly enough, with a funny nickname, but it doesn't stop there. Next she'll make fun of your clothes or your hair, the way you talk, your family, your religion or anything about you that is different. You start to feel as if there is something really wrong with you.

Picture the scene: On the bus to school the joker and her friends have been picking on a girl who doesn't seem to have any friends. Do you:

1. Ignore the situation?

2. Join in?

3. Tell the joker to stop and taunt her back?

4. Grab a seat next to the girl and talk to her. When the taunting starts, act like it doesn't bother you?

If you chose number one, sticking your head in the sand is no way to deal with life. If you chose number two, you spend too much time trying to please other people. Try being yourself. If you chose number three, you're one tough cookie, but sometimes challenging the teaser sets up even more trouble. If you chose number four, you are making a positive difference and finding ways to stop the taunting.

◇ Coping with the joker

The joker doesn't feel good about herself. Perhaps she's been a victim of taunting and is trying to drag others down to where she feels she is. Remember that anyone who belittles or humiliates someone else is feeling empty inside.

 Mean words can cut you to the quick. You do not have to put up with them. If you do, jokers will just pick and taunt more. The first time you get teased you can respond with a 'funny, ha, ha'. If it happens again, you can tell them they said that already and ask if anything is wrong or if they are okay. If it happens for the third time, write down what was said, and then carry a notebook with you. They are bound to ask you what you are doing, and you can say you are writing about the things they are saying about you. They'll laugh at first, but it will also make them think twice. You could even go so far as to carry a tape recorder so you can record the bad words, slurs and names. But if the teasing gets out of control and your tactics don't work, it's crucial you talk to your parents or a teacher you trust.

As hurtful as teasing can be, try to
remember that cruel words have
meaning only if you let them. The
joker is picking on you so she can
feel better about herself, and if you

let it get you down you're giving her what she wants.
If you aren't being teased, support someone who is.
Teasing can spread through your school like a wildfire.
Stamp it out. The girl being teased may look like she
isn't upset, but believe me, she is. Be strong, stick-up
for each other and you'll be able to stand up to the
joker with ease.

⬦ And if you are the joker...

We all tease people sometimes, and it's fine if the
kidding is good-natured and nobody gets hurt. But
there is a fine line between kidding and taunting or
bullying. If you find yourself teasing others in a cruel
way, maybe it's because you aren't feeling very good

about yourself, but that's no reason to take it out on others. Stop it right away. Apologise to those you have hurt. Turn your mean words into nice words. Find something good to say to those around you. You'll be amazed how much better you feel about yourself, and how much other people warm to you, when you look for the good in them.

Chapter eight

The
wannabe,
the torn bystander,
the target and the spirit

Hopefully the last few chapters have given you some insight into the main types of mean girl behaviour and some pointers on how to deal with it. Now we'll take a look at four roles, which are just as common but not quite so easy to define as types. That's because almost all girls (including you) slip in and out of them at various times.

✧ The Wannabe

Almost all girls are wannabes or pleasers at some time or other. The wannabe can be popular or unpopular. She's out to please the person who is the flavour of the moment. She acts differently when she's hanging around with different people, and this can cause problems. When she's with an It girl she mimics her clothes or style. When she's with a bully she becomes her sidekick. When she's with the gossip – you guessed it – she becomes a gossip. She tries hard to fit in and she often ends up going between two groups of girls who are mad at each other. Being a go-between gives her a lot of power, and instead of helping both sides get over their problems, she may just try to keep them mad with each other so they all stay friends with her.

To the wannabe, what other people want is more important than what she wants. Her opinions change according to the person she is with. She does things to please people and is desperate to have the right look and fit in.

Playing the role of the wannabe means that you haven't really figured out who you are or what you want. You feel insecure about your friendships and never know if girls like you because of who you are or because you do what they want. In short, you need a boost of self-confidence.

Every girl feels like this sometimes, but being a people pleaser is no way to win friendships or feel happy about yourself. Whenever you catch yourself starting to care too much about whether someone likes you, remember that this is never going to make you happy. Worrying about what other people think is no way to live your life, it's what *you* think that matters.

◇ The Torn Bystander

Every girl (including you) takes on the role of the torn bystander now and again. The torn bystander wants

to do the right thing, but she also wants to go along with her friends. Her good side means that she wants everyone to get along. She recognises wrongdoing when she sees it – and that means she has bags of potential. Her bad side means that she isn't good at saying no to her friends, and when she sees wrongdoing she feels powerless to stop it.

Playing the role of the torn bystander means that you're giving up a lot. You may not try new things, or you may stop doing things because your friends make fun of you. You probably play your strengths down so that you can get along with others. Lots of clever girls hide their intelligence for fear that other girls – and

boys – won't like them. Maybe you cover up your true personality from your girlfriends for fear of losing them. If you do, it's time to ask yourself why on earth you want to hang around with people who don't accept you for who you are.

◇ The Target

She's the victim, set up by other girls to be gossiped about, humiliated, excluded or laughed at. She might be the class loser, but sometimes she's the one in a

group of girls who hasn't gone along with everyone else or who has had the courage to stand up for herself. She feels helpless to stop the mean girl and she feels bad that others are rejecting her for no good reason. She

can become so anxious that she feels sick to her stomach and can't concentrate on her schoolwork. She feels she has no allies and no one to back her up, and sometimes she covers up her feelings by rejecting other people first, saying she doesn't like anyone.

The target role can be hell to deal with but, believe it or not, there are hidden benefits. There's nothing like being a target to teach you about understanding and respect for the feelings of others. If you know what

it's like to be picked on, you're far more likely to champion the underdog who's being unfairly treated by your friends. Being a

target can also give you a new view of the world. You can see the cost of fitting in and decide that sometimes you're better off on the outside, where you can be true to yourself and find true friends. If this sounds too scary, don't panic. There are loads of girls out there who would love to be your friend. All you need to do is follow the advice in chapter twelve to find real friends who like you for who you are.

◇ The Spirit

The spirit is easy to spot because she doesn't hang around with any one group of girls. She has friends in different groups and moves freely among them. She likes herself and doesn't depend on being liked by a group. She is nice to everyone and doesn't exclude 'losers'. She's confident and doesn't need to sacrifice herself in order to be popular. She doesn't rule by meanness or feel the need to make others uncomfortable or insecure. Because she is her own person, she is genuinely liked and respected for who she is.

In every girl there is a spirit who wants to get out. Read on. We're going to set her free.

Chapter nine

Girl wars

So far you've seen how teasing, gossip and mean girl behaviour can make you afraid to be who you really are. Now let's take a look at how you can make a difference in real-life situations. We'll explore several typical power plays and offer advice on how to stand up for yourself and get support from your friends.

◇ Power Plays

Assembly has just finished, and the girls file out towards their lockers where they will hang around for a few minutes before the bell rings. Linda walks to her locker, expecting her usual chat with Sonia, Mary and Wendy.

When she arrives they fall silent and refuse to look her in the eye. Sonia looks anxious, and Mary and Wendy look away.

Linda: 'Hi guys, what's the gossip?'

Sonia: 'Nothing. We should go. The bell is about to ring.'

Linda: 'Let's catch up first break, right?'
Sonia: 'Um.'

Wendy: (silence)

Mary: 'Come on, Sonia and Wendy, time to go.'

Linda watches them walk away without her. What has she done wrong?

If this happens to you, believe me, you're not alone.
Every girl experiences this kind of power play at some
point in her school life. One day you are best friends,
and the next day things are different.

It's wonderful to have best mates you can giggle with, walk arm-in-arm with, share your secrets with, go to parties and sleepovers with and have long phone calls with. But along with the joy goes the flip side: being excluded from parties and isolated from the group, or suddenly being ignored by a best friend and feeling heartbroken.

So what can you do?

If you're Linda: why are you hanging around with girls who treat you this way? This isn't friendship. Friends are people who make you feel good not bad. It's going to be tough if you've hung around with these girls for years but this could be your chance to leave the old behind and make some real friends. Hang in there, because later in the book you'll find ways to do this.

If you're Mary or Sonia: despite looking as if you are in control in this scenario you are actually the ones most lacking in

confidence. It's often the case that the girls who try to exclude others, or make them feel unwanted, are feeling deeply insecure themselves. It's time for you to really work on building your self-esteem and to start treating your friends with kindness and respect. Chapter twelve is a must-read for you. Otherwise you may wake up one day to find that your greatest fear has come true – nobody wants to hang around with you!

If you're Wendy: you can't bring yourself to speak in this scenario suggesting that you are uncomfortable with the exclusion. You know something isn't right but you are afraid of being excluded by Mary and Sonia so you offer your friend no support. What you need to ask yourself is: why are you hanging around with people who expect you to go along with things you know are wrong? Even though you are sitting on the fence in this scenario your self-esteem is just as low as Mary's and Sonia's and you, like them, need to learn what real friendship is all about.

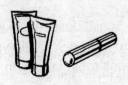

◇ The Party Rejection

Nothing can be worse than not being invited to a friend's party. You just want to hide away and never come out. Parties aren't about the presents or the cake. No, they are about deciding, in consultation with your best friends, who to invite and who to leave out. And if you invite boys, things get even more exciting, and complicated.

Jo: 'Did you get your invite?'

Lucy: 'To what?'

Jo: 'You know, Florence's party.'
Lucy: 'Um. I'm not sure. I'll let you know.'

The next day:

Jo: 'Really sorry, Lucy, but I chatted with Florence, and she's only allowed to invite ten of her closest friends.'

Lucy: 'That's okay.'

Jo: 'Would you like me to talk to her and see if she'll invite you too?'

Right now Lucy is feeling rejected, at the bottom of
the pile and wondering why Florence doesn't like her.
Jo is feeling important – she gets to be in the middle.
She's also feeling torn because she wants to help her
friend but wants to go to the party too. Florence is
just enjoying being the centre of attention and having
control over others.

What can you do?

 If you're Florence: obviously it's your big
day and you want to invite your special
friends, but why make other girls feel
bad in the process? How would you feel if it
happened to you? If for some good reason you can't
open up your party, be sensitive to the girls you don't
invite. Put your invitation in the post so girls won't be
opening them at school and the
ones who weren't invited will be
spared the questions. Keep things
low-key and perhaps tell the girls

you didn't invite that sometime soon you'd like to get together with them and have some fun – say a shopping trip or a cinema visit.

If you're Jo: figure out what you're getting out of this. Are you in the middle of things because you feel bad that Lucy wasn't invited or because the situation makes you feel like the star of the show? If it's the latter, you're trying to be popular instead of paying attention to other people's feelings. If it's the former, do you want to go to a party where your best friend is excluded? If you do decide to go, make a point of reassuring your friend that even though you are going to the party her friendship is very important to you, and plan ahead to do something with her.

If you're Lucy: of course you're going to feel low, but it's impossible to be everyone's best friend. Plan a treat for yourself on the day of the party to remind yourself that there is more to life than your school friends. Do not try to hint at wanting an invitation – you'll just feel like you're begging. As painful as being excluded is, it's much more empowering to be able to cope with and rise above these things.

◇ Threesomes and Tag-a-longs

Francesca and Henrietta are very good friends. Sometimes they hang around with Nina, who used to be Francesca's best friend, but Francesca prefers Henrietta now because she is more interested in boys. Francesca and Henrietta decide to go the cinema together. Nina overhears and asks if she can come. Henrietta tells Nina she is a tag-a-long and she should make her own friends. Francesca feels sorry for Nina but doesn't say anything.

Right now Nina is hurt by the other girl's rejection. She's just trying to fit in. Francesca feels torn between her new friendship and doing the right thing, and Henrietta wants to put Nina in her place.

What can you do?

If you're Nina: ask yourself why you want to hang around with girls who clearly don't want you around. Is being part of a group more important to you than friendship? Face it, Francesca has every right to have her own interests and hang around with girls who share them. You could try getting her on her own and telling her how her actions make you feel. If the outcome is bad, it might be time to accept that the friendship is either on a downer and you need to give each other space, or that it is ending. If that's the case feel proud of yourself – you have done nothing wrong. Remember that you can make new friends who you will probably be happier with in the end.

If you're Henrietta: there's a lot you can learn about yourself from this experience. There's nothing wrong with wanting to spend time with a particular friend alone, but that doesn't give you any right to treat someone else as you did. It doesn't matter how you feel about Nina, it's wrong to be cruel. What is it about Nina that you don't like? Why do you feel the need to be rude to her? Why are you putting Francesca in the middle like that? How would you feel if the tables were turned and you were being excluded? Take responsibility for your behaviour, stop hurting people and apologise to both your friends.

If you're Francesca: stop thinking that your bad behaviour towards your friend is all Henrietta's fault and take responsibility for your actions.

You do have the right to choose your own friends, but you don't have the right to make anyone else feel like dirt in the process. What you did was understandable.

Perhaps you felt vulnerable and didn't want to get on Henrietta's wrong side, but do you want to be the kind of girl who is pushed around by her friends? Do you want to be the person who says nothing when another person is bullied? The best thing you can do is apologise to Nina in front of Henrietta and say you didn't feel right about what happened.

◇ The Letdowns

Nicky and Jo are in year 10, and they used to hang around with each other all the time, but recently they have started to become friends with different groups. Nicky and Jo plan to have a sleepover on Saturday, but a few hours before Nicky leaves for Jo's house one of Nicky's new friends asks her to go to the cinema. She also tells Nicky a couple of really cute boys from school want to go with them.

What would you do if you were Nicky?

I've asked this question many times to several year 9 classes, and only three girls have ever stuck to their plans with Jo. A few more said they would ask if Jo could come too, but a whopping majority said they would lie and come up with some reason why they couldn't go to the sleepover. Whatever choice you make, you are learning important lessons:

✦ If you stick to your original plan, you may feel disappointed and angry.

✦ If you lie and let Jo down, you'll probably feel guilty and confused.

✦ If you ask Jo to come along too, you run the risk of upsetting your new friend or your new friend might be mean to Jo.

If you're in this kind of no-win situation, what is the best thing to do? Okay, your new friend may seem more exciting, but you need to keep any commitments you make, regardless of whether a better offer comes along. If you feel like you can't say no, think about whether you are being yourself with your new friend or whether you are changing your

personality to suit her. If your new friend is someone worth holding on to, she'll respect your loyalty and arrange another time. If you did ask Jo to come along and your new friend was upset about it or mean to Jo, you need to think about whether you want to be with a friend who is so controlling.

⬦ Best friends forever – or for a day?

Do you have a best friend who you just can't live without? Perhaps you wear each other's clothes or have crushes on the same person or like the same kind of music. You share everything and can't imagine life without each other.

Then you make up, break up, make up... and so on. Sometimes you are dumped; sometimes you're the dumper. When you break up you hate her, but when you are back together you couldn't be happier. And this can happen not just with one friend but with a group of friends.

One day you go to school and the group of friends you partied with at the weekend has decided that you are no longer one of them and there isn't room for you at the table during lunch. Sometimes there's a reason – perhaps you talked to the wrong person at the party or left too early. Sometimes there just isn't a reason except that the others have decided you don't belong anymore.

However it happens, it's devastating. You come away learning that girls – even the ones you think are your best friends – can turn on you on a whim. As hard as it is, there is something positive that you can get from it. The painful experience can also teach you the true meaning of friendship which is something we'll explore later in the book.

It's confusing and painful when friends exclude you and you'll probably be wracking your brains to find out why you are suddenly on the outside. You think that there has to be a reason and you wonder whether you did something wrong. But as you'll see in the next two chapters, your fall from grace isn't about being wrong or right or being a good or bad person, it's about superficial things such as the way you look, the clothes you wear and the boys you fancy.

CHAPTER TEN

Looking good

Is there anything more frightening than a scornful 'what are you wearing' from your friends? It's crucial to fit in and to look the same. You announce to the world who's in and who's not by what you are wearing. And as if looking right wasn't tough enough, this is the time when your body starts to do crazy, unpredictable things – your breasts grow, you get body hair, spots, hips and periods.

◇ Curves in all the right places

Remember the girl who developed first? Remember the stir it caused – the comments from boys and girls?

'There's this girl in my class with huge breasts. Everyone talks about them, and she enjoys the attention. The girls call her a tart because she's all over the boys and the boys are all over her, but secretly they are envious. We sometimes make fun of her by stuffing socks down our bras. I wonder if a boy likes her for her, or for her bust?'
Carla, 13

If you developed early, you may feel self-conscious and do all you can to hide your body, especially if you hang around with girls who haven't developed. Of course, if you haven't developed and all your friends have, you may be wondering what's wrong with you.

Whether you worry about having curves in the right places or weighing too much or too little, the chances are that no matter how beautiful you are, you probably don't think you are. The beauty standards of Girl World are ruthless. You can't win! You notice all your flaws and are sure everyone else notices them too. If you don't believe you're ugly, you're sure your friends will think you're conceited.

So what are you to do?
Unfortunately, people will always
judge others by the way they look
so it's something that you will find
hard to ignore. But you don't have to believe other
people or worry so much about what they think of the
way you look. You can walk through life believing in
your self-worth. Feeling good about who you are on
the inside will make you look confident and attractive
on the outside.

◇ How to survive

Whatever you do, don't be the girl
everyone likes because she puts herself
down. You don't have to flatter others by
telling them they are much prettier,
cleverer or funnier than you are. It might protect you
from the teasing of other girls, but it's degrading and
destroys your self-esteem. It's not worth it!

How about those low-slung jeans or
tight tops your mum probably hates
you wearing? If you want to wear
something that your mum won't like,
have a think about what your
motivation is. When you wear tight

87

tops, you have to know that some people may think
you are trying to draw their attention to your body.
You may think you just look pretty, but others may
think you are trying to get their attention. Be aware of
what messages you're sending. Are you confident
enough to be yourself no matter what you wear?

People without confidence rely on their clothes to feel good about themselves. Confident people rely on their inner strength, not their outfits, to feel happy.

 It's the same with shaving your legs, plucking your eyebrows and wearing makeup. You may think it's all very grown-up, but if you don't feel grown-up on the inside, you might just be putting on an act and people will see through that.

What about body shape and periods? How do you cope when you're teased because of having (or not having) breasts? First of all, other girls tease anyone who looks different to them. Bodies come in all shapes and sizes, and they are all beautiful in their own way. Remember that you are not the only one. Other girls – maybe in other classes or other schools – are feeling just the way you are. Getting periods is normal, and it happens to everyone (no matter how embarrassing you think it is). If you don't know what is happening or you are too embarrassed to ask questions, buy a book that explains everything. Look in the Useful Contacts section on page 123 for some web sites and books that can help.

If you long to be thinner, think about why thinner is supposed to be better. The photos of models you see in magazines are airbrushed; they don't look like that in real life. The body images they advertise are unhealthy. Do these pictures make you feel good about yourself? If they don't, why on earth are you trying to be like these girls?

Have a think. When do you give in and fit into what others think is beautiful, and when do you go for it  and stand on your own? You may wonder why standing on your own is so important. Well, the more you stand on your own, the stronger you grow emotionally. You will become a person in your own right, not a crowd pleaser.

Yes, it's true, being grown-up isn't about doing what everyone else thinks is cool; it's about finding what works for you and only you. It's about being yourself.

◇ Don't judge a book by its cover

Just as it doesn't work to value yourself by the way
you look, try not to form an opinion of others by the
way they look. Why? Because you're probably wrong.
Ever had a laugh with a mate about
the way someone else looks?
Hopefully, after hearing the stories
below you might think next time
before you speak.

Anna, 13: 'They call me Specky-Four-Eyes.'

Words from the gossip:
   'Look at her. She looks like a right geek.'

What Anna says:
   'I found out I was long-sighted five years ago, and
   that's when I started wearing glasses.
   Straightaway people looked at me differently.
   Then in junior school I got my nickname. I tried
   to ignore it, but it really upset me. I'd love to
   wear contacts one day, but I'm
   not going to let anyone bully
   me into it.'

Polly, 12: 'I'm ashamed to smile.'

Words from the gossip:
'She always looks so moody.'

What Polly says:
'Every time I smile I really feel self-conscious because I hate my teeth. They are really crooked, and I think they look horrible when I smile – especially now I'm wearing braces. When I was younger people used to call me Bugs Bunny. Since then I've always looked away when I smile so my ugly teeth aren't so noticeable.'

Amber, 13: 'I like dressing in black.'

Words from the gossip:
'She's a freak.'

What Amber says:
'I was picked on a lot in secondary school for having acne, so to draw attention from that I started to dress in black all the time. Instead of picking on me for my skin, people started to make comments about the colour I was wearing, but I found that easier to take. Just because I wear black doesn't make me a freak. I'm still the same me on the inside.'

Just because someone looks a teeny bit different on the outside doesn't mean that they aren't worth getting to know. So why not see what they are like on the inside before you judge them. Think of everyone as a friend you haven't met yet. Nothing is abnormal because everyone is different. Life would be so boring if we were all the same. Before forming an opinion of someone, go and chat to them. Find out a bit more about them and you may be surprised by how well you get on.

Chapter eleven

Girl meets boy

◆◆◆ 'I'm obsessed with this guy called Peter. I'm not
sure why, and I'm not sure if he even knows I
like him. Every day at break time me and my
friends hang around where he plays football
and we all count the number of times he looks
our way.'
Cindy, 13

Life can get exciting when you start to have
crushes. Is there anything more thrilling than
whispering with your girlfriends about who you've got
your eye on?

When you start to fancy a boy, what's the
first thing you do? You tell your girlfriend.
You report every word or every glance
from the boy to her. In fact, you probably
spend more time talking to your girlfriend
about your 'boyfriend' than to the boy
himself. In the early stages of a romance,
your girlfriends are your best support.

But what if you are being egged on by your girlfriends
when you don't really want a boyfriend yet? Or the

boy they decided suits you perfectly
leaves you cold? What if your best
friend has a crush on the boy you
are after? Suddenly the world that
seemed cozy when you had your
girlfriends to fall back on starts to
feel nasty instead. There is nothing that unites or
divides Girl World as much as boys.

✧ Take things slowly

Just as you can feel anxious if you
aren't developing physically at the
same time as your girlfriends, you'll

feel out of sync if you're boy crazy
and your friends aren't or if they're
boy mad and you couldn't care less.
The important thing to remember,
when it comes to your feelings and
emotions, is that nothing is abnormal.

If your friends are caught up in the boy frenzy it's
easy to feel pressure to act that way too. You may
get teased if you hang around with boys as friends
when your friends think you should have a boyfriend.

It's up to you to decide when you
are ready to start going out with
boys. You don't have to behave in a
certain way or go out with someone just because
your friends want you to. Take a deep breath. Take
things slowly. And don't ever forget that what your
friends want, or what boys want, is never more
important than what YOU want or feel to be right.

◇ Fighting over boys

Getting a boy's attention may become more and more important to you as you get older. You could find yourself acting differently, like flirting around boys or even sacrificing your friendships with girls. Perhaps you've been hurt by a girlfriend who has lied or backstabbed to get the boy she wants. Perhaps you've fought with your friend over a boy, or perhaps your friend has made it clear that when boys are around you take second place.

Picture the scene: you make plans to hang around with your friends at someone's house, then 'he' calls and all plans are off. Sadly, Girl World often values boyfriends over anything else, and many girls just accept it, even if they don't like it. It's a rare girl who can stand up and tell a girlfriend how hurt she is for being dumped for a boy.

By secondary school your friendships with other girls may be made or broken over boys. You could even  become so mistrustful of other girls that you shrink your circle of friends, confiding in just a few or none at all.

Getting together with another girl's boyfriend is the
most common cause of conflict. Stealing a boyfriend
violates the most sacred trust between girls. But
when it happens, girls usually let the boy off the
hook. Rarely do they blame the boy as much as the
girl. They excuse boys' behaviour, but they don't
excuse girls'. The result is that over time girls trust

each other less and less and turn more and more to boys for support. The danger here is that the focus shifts from pleasing your friends to pleasing boys – and sometimes that need to please can become desperate. Here are some steps you can take to make sure it never goes that far.

◇ Positive relationship pointers

✦ Respect your friendships with boys and girls alike. It isn't right to reject someone when a better offer comes along, even if that offer is the love of your life. If you told this 'better offer' you had already made plans to see your girlfriend and he got angry, you need to think about why you want to go out with anyone who doesn't want you to have your own life.

✦ Go at your own pace as far as boys are concerned. You don't need a boyfriend to be cool or to fit in if your friends all have one.

✦ You don't always have to be 'nice' when boys are around. It's okay to be grumpy, to tell a boy you aren't interested or to simply be yourself.

✦ If any boy is harassing or intimidating you always go to your parents or a teacher for help.

✦ If you feel inferior to your boyfriend or he isn't treating you right, you don't have to take it. Relationships should be based on mutual love,  respect and equality. A good relationship makes you happy. If your boyfriend makes you cry more than he makes you laugh, get out of there.

✦ If you feel really shy around boys, forget about them and focus on other things. Build your confidence in other areas: your schoolwork, a part-time job, your hobby and so on. You may just find that when you stop obsessing about boys they start noticing you more.

There's nothing more appealing to a boy than a girl who believes in herself and has her own life and interests. This may take several years to happen, but that's nothing to worry about. As far as boys are concerned, the best advice is always to take it slowly and be true to yourself.

Chapter twelve

Real friends

Anna's thirteenth birthday is only a day away when her two best friends inform her that they won't be coming to her sleepover party after all. 'Tina asked us to go to the cinema with her. That's way more fun than watching DVDs at your house and playing those stupid games your mum comes up with,' they snicker, linking arms and walking away.

Lucy is eleven and hates break time when a boy will sneak up and snap the back of her new bra. Worse yet are her friends, who cluster together and laugh when it happens.

With friends like these, who needs enemies? What do you think is going on here? Is this real friendship? No, it certainly is not!

◇ Friends versus cliques

If you are like Anna and Lucy, hanging around with friends that make you unhappy, it's time to make changes. But where do you begin? The first step is to stay away from girls who belong to a clique.

Is there a difference between a group of girlfriends and a clique? There certainly is. But first take a look at some of the things cliques and groups of friends have in common.

Being part of a group of friends can help you learn to get along with others. It gives you the chance to have fun with other girls and get close to them. You learn about each other and learn to trust each other.

But there's a really BIG difference between cliques and a group of real friends. Cliques tend to make members conform. This means you

have to think, act, talk and dress like
everyone else in the clique. You may
even end up doing the strangest
things to belong – things you don't
feel comfortable with, such as smoking
or lying about how much money you have. The
result? You might feel like a phoney; having to be the
way other people want you to be just to have friends.
If you don't conform, like Anna who wanted to have a
girls' night in instead of a night out at the cinema or
Lucy who felt uncomfortable in her new bra, you can
feel excluded or left out.

◇ What are real girlfriends?

Real girlfriends like the real you and you
like the real them. You don't have to
impress them or be phoney around them.
That's the great thing about real friends. They accept
who you are. They're there for you when you're upset
or have a problem. They keep your secrets and know
what makes you laugh. Best of all, they care about
you and you care about them. Are
your friends real friends, or are you
hanging out with the wrong girls?
Ask yourself these questions:

✦ Do I feel like I have to behave in a certain way to be accepted?

✦ Do I feel like a fake?

✦ Does the group try to keep me from making other friends?

✦ Do I feel like I always have to get the approval of others in the group?

✦ Do I feel out of place in the group?

✦ Would I let down a friend if something better came along?

✦ Do I find it hard to tell my friends when I don't want to go along with what they want, and do they ignore what I am saying?

If you answered yes to any one of
these questions, you might want
to really consider what friendship
and commitment mean to you. If
you pretend to be someone you are not then you are
setting yourself up for unhappiness and insecurity.
But it doesn't have to be that way. When you face
cliques and friendship problems, you can use the
experience to help you figure out why it is so vital to
be true to yourself – however scary or impossible it
 may seem at the time – and to think
through what real friendship is all about.

◇ How to make real friends

When you feel let down, ask yourself the golden
question: is this how a real friend would treat me?
Think about what you want and need in a friendship.
Write a list of what qualities you want in a friend.
Most of us want friends we can trust, friends who are
reliable and honest, and friends who respect us for
who we are. Do your friends
show you these things? If they
don't, then you have to think long
and hard about why you have
these friends.

If you do decide that your friends aren't right for you, this can be a lonely and hard time. You have to be really strong to break up with a friend because you don't feel respected, but it could be one of the best things you ever do. Choosing what is right for you helps you to develop self-esteem. This means liking yourself as you are, and it's the key to success in life.

If you've decided that it's time to find other friends who let you just be you then you may be feeling a rising sense of panic, but take a deep breath. Finding new friends really isn't as scary or impossible as you think. The friendship pointers below will help you every step of the way.

◇ Friendship pointers

If you want to make new friends, you have to look for them. You won't meet anyone if you stay inside all

day watching TV. Maybe your friends don't have to go to the same school as you. Maybe they don't have to be the same age, gender or race.

You'll be amazed how much you can learn from people who aren't like you. Start by making a point of talking to the new girl.

When meeting someone new, just say something friendly like, 'I love your shoes' or 'do you know what tonight's homework is?' Keep practising, and it will get easier. Try to make other people feel good. Ask questions to show that you are interested in them such as, 'I've noticed you're really good at art.' And remember to listen to their answers. Hear what they have to say, and show them that you understand.

Don't try to hog the limelight; you'll only
drive people away. Invite a few people
to join you for lunch or, if it's okay with
your parents, to come to your house
after school.

One great way to meet new friends is to join a club,
start a new hobby or an activity that's outside school.
School may seem huge right now but there's a whole
world outside and lots of great people waiting to get
to know you.

Friendships don't just happen and you can't
force them, so don't overdo it. Take your
time. It's something you can work on every
day by being friendly. Smile and say hello to
people a lot, find something nice to say to
at least one person each day, help people out if you
can and have a laugh with people. In other words, be
kind, generous and cheerful – and never be afraid to
be you.

◇ Being popular

 Being popular can be fun, but don't make the mistake of thinking it is more important than your family, your schoolwork, your hobbies, your goals and most of all, your opinion of yourself.

Do you want to hear something surprising? When you say you want to be popular, what you really want isn't to have masses of friends. What you really want is to feel good about yourself.

Feeling happy with yourself is something you can work on by turning negative thoughts about yourself into positive ones. Start by asking how popular you are with yourself. If you base your self-esteem on what other people think of you, you'll always feel insecure, but learning to like yourself – now, that's the real secret of popularity.

Stop worrying about what other girls want you to do, and start being yourself. Why strive so hard to be like everyone else? Be extraordinary. If a faddy dress code is gripping the school, step back. Fads never last.

111

You're in charge. Be what you want, be the person you like. Just make sure you are being true to yourself.

◇ Your friendship strategy

Before getting involved in any group, be sure to ask yourself what makes the girls in the group tick. If the group isn't genuine and is just for show, step back and think before you dive in. If it's for true friendship then embrace it. Here's a friendship strategy to help you on the road to finding real friends:

✦ Acknowledge the pressure that your friends can put you under and your fear of being unpopular.

✦ Think about why your friends behave the way they do and why you behave the way that you do.

112

✦ If you make mistakes or get it wrong, admit it to them.

✦ Always keep in mind the qualities you want in a new friend: trust, reliability, honesty and respect, and make sure that you are the sort of friend who has these qualities.

✦ Every friendship has its ups and downs, so be patient with your friends. A real friendship is worth the effort.

◇ If people still exclude you...

What do you do if, no matter how friendly you are, people still snub you? You may feel sad and alone, but you do have a choice about how to handle the situation. Don't ignore them, try to get your own back or try to impress them. Instead, try something very powerful indeed. Dare to be different!

Being different doesn't mean you are weird or unpopular, it means you are an independent thinker – an individual. It means you believe you are an interesting, worthwhile person with or without the 'in' crowd.

How do you learn to be an individual? You start by believing in yourself, and that's what the last chapter is all about.

Chapter thirteen

Girl power

Never forget that you are unique. There never has and never will be another person on this earth just like you. Doesn't that make you feel special and original? Remind yourself every day that you are one of a kind. Enjoy your originality. Whenever you feel the urge to merge with the crowd, pause for a while to think about how special you are. Celebrate your differences because they are what make you a precious person with your own unique place in the world.

You're far more powerful than you think. If you are the victim of mean girl behaviour or if you know it exists in your school, you really can make a

difference, starting right now. How? By treating other girls the way you want to be treated and finding friends who feel the same way.

◇ All it takes is one girl

'When I started year 8 all the girls picked on me or wouldn't hang around with me because I was bigger than they were. I also didn't have a clue about fashion or why being thin seemed to matter so much. They said so many mean things. I had to learn how to stand up for myself. Now I always try to be myself and not give in to worrying about what others think. I'm still big, but this hasn't dented my self-esteem. Most importantly of all, I stay away from girls who say mean things about me and other people, and I hang around with people who are positive. In the end it has worked. I'm happy.'
Jill, 17

From now on I want you to focus on yourself and all the things that you can do to promote girl power.
Here are some tips:

116

✦ Be sure to do your best with your schoolwork. Set yourself goals. Ask your teacher for help. Think long-term. In ten years' time it's the grades and school references that will matter, not who is in or out of the 'in' crowd.

✦ Think more about your life outside school. School may seem huge to you at the moment, but it really is a very small cog in the wheel. There's a whole world out there waiting for you to explore it. What are you doing when you are not at school? Make sure you have fun.

✦ How about helping other girls, or other people, perhaps in your school or in the community? When things aren't going well it's easy to think that nobody has ever had it so bad, but there will always be people worse off than you. Everyone appreciates a kind word or some help – from the new girl in school to the old woman who lives down your street.

✦ If you don't like the way you are acting or if you find yourself lashing out at other people, talk to your teacher, the school counsellor or your parents about your problems. If you don't feel comfortable with that then call the confidential phone lines listed in the Useful Contacts section on page 123. This will help you see that you aren't alone. You'll learn that you are stronger than you think. You'll be able to see where your sadness is coming from. Perhaps your parents are divorcing or you've lost a loved one or you can't keep up with schoolwork. It will also help you realise that taking it out on your classmates just isn't going to make it any better. Asking for help will mean you can find the courage to work it out without hurting other people.

✦ If you're being picked on because of your weight and you aren't eating healthy foods or exercising, why not try to make some healthy changes? You'll find helpful books and web sites in the

Useful Contacts section. A healthy body and a healthy mind go hand in hand. Why not start taking better care of yourself? Don't do it because you are being picked on but because you deserve to look and feel your best.

✦ To help everyone think about the difference between harmless banter and hateful words, you may want to ask your teacher for a lesson that

promotes girl-to-girl friendships and awareness of mean girl behaviour. Perhaps you and your friends could think up some rules that you want to discuss with your class. For example, bullying isn't cool. Standing back and watching someone get bullied means you are a bully too, and so on. Why not suggest to your friends that you have a no-gossiping-teasing-bullying-other-girls day every week? Why not ask a teacher you like to see if some rules about mean girl behaviour can be included in the school handbook? You and your

friends can be the ones who play a part in getting the message out that it's wrong to be mean and unkind.

✦ Why not start a newcomers club for
girls starting at school? Use this club
to discuss how to make every girl
enjoy school more. Think of all the things you can
do to make your school less unkind, and think
how many girls you can help in this way. These
kinds of discussions will empower you – and
they'll empower your friends and all the other
girls at your school too. Create a group that
everyone can join. Offering this kind of support
can make a huge positive change for other girls.

✦ Talk about how powerful girls can be. Realise that
it is okay to be different and that these
differences make you stronger rather than

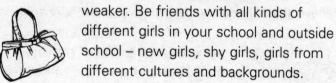

weaker. Be friends with all kinds of
different girls in your school and outside
school – new girls, shy girls, girls from
different cultures and backgrounds.

✦ Keep working on your friendships. Show your
friends kindness and respect, stick up for them,
support them when they need help, tell them the
truth in a kind way, say you're sorry when you've
messed up, be forgiving when they mess up and
keep promises and commitments even if a so-
called better offer comes up. Never try to change

your friends. Accept them for who they are, and always be thankful for your friends. In short, treat them the way you want them to treat you.

◇ Greatness is in you

Don't think you don't have the courage to do all of this. Of course you do! You can and you will make a difference. All it takes is one girl to start a positive trend and others will soon follow. Use the power of your mind. Imagine yourself being respected by your friends and being surrounded by kindness. Imagine yourself doing well at school and succeeding in life. Believe that you can accomplish whatever you want.

Greatness is in you every time you think things through, listen to your heart and try the best that you can. Sometimes doing the right thing – being upbeat, generous and biting your tongue – seems like the tough choice and isn't half as much fun as a good old gossip or doing what everyone else is doing. But let mean girl behaviour stop with you. You know how harmful it can be. Make the change you want to see. Help yourself, and help other girls change a toxic atmosphere into a supportive one.

By reading this book, you have given yourself so many new and exciting choices. Now that you know how to spot mean girl behaviour, learn from it and handle it, there is nothing you can't do if you put your mind to it.

Hopefully you have learned more about the courageous and wonderful person you are. You are your own girl and you have the power to be you because you are learning to think things through, make choices and not be influenced by the way others behave. You are learning that you can make changes happen and that one girl – you – can make a difference. You are learning to do your best and to be proud of the unique woman you will soon become.

Useful information and contacts

✧ Films

Here are some good films for Girl World analysis. I'm sure you can think of more recent ones to add:

Clueless
Never Been Kissed
Ten things I Hate About You
She's All That
Mean Girls

◇ Magazines to celebrate girl power

Mizz
27th Floor, King's Reach Tower, Stamford Street
London SE1 9LS
E-mail: mizz@ipcmedia.com

Girl Talk
Room A1130, Woodlands, 80 Wood Lane
London W12 OTT
E-mail: girltalk.magazine@bbc.co.uk

◇ Further reading

The Girls' Book of Wisdom
　　ed. Catherine Dee (Megan Tingley Books, 1999)

The Girls' Guide to Life: How to Take Charge of the Issues that Affect You
　　by Catherine Dee (Little Brown, 1997)

GirlWise: How to be Confident, Capable, Cool and in Control
　　by Julia De Villers (Prima Publishing, 2002)

Wise Guides: Periods
  by Charlotte Owen (Hodder Children's Books, 2005)

Wise Guides: Self-esteem/Eating
  both by Anita Naik (Hodder Children's Books, 2005)

Wise Guides: Bullying
  by Michele Elliott (Hodder Children's Books, 2005)

✧ Confidential helplines and advisory centres for teenagers

BROOK ADVISORY CENTRES
  For advice on emotional and sexual health issues.
  Tel: 08000 185023 for your local number.

CARELINE
  Confidential telephone counselling for young people on any issue, including family and relationship problems, bullying, child abuse, eating disorders, bereavement, addictions, rape, depression and anxiety.
  Tel: 0208 514 1177 (Mon-Fri 10 am–4 pm and 7–10 pm)

CHILDLINE

A 24-hour helpline for young people, offering advice on any issue from friendship to puberty.
Tel 0800 1111

THE SAMARITANS

A 24-hour free emotional support helpline for anyone going through a crisis.
Tel: 08457 90 90 90 (local numbers are listed inside the front cover of local phone books).

YOUTH ACCESS

Will put you in touch with local contacts for counselling advice and information.
Tel: 0208 772 9900
(9.30 am–5.30 pm Mon-Fri, answerphone)

◇ Useful web sites

This is a short list, but many of these sites offer links to other sites.

www.gurl.com
> Contains lots of interesting info for teenage girls.

http://atdpweb.soe.berkeley.edu/quest/home.html
> A site to help you learn about yourself, career options and positive female role models.

www.beinggirl.com
> A fun way to learn about reproduction.

http://www.girlspace.com
> Tips on self-esteem and coping with growing up stuff.

http://www.teenadvice.org/
> Ask a question and you'll get advice.

Index